Waffen-SS

(1)Forging an Army (1934-1943)

Robert Michulec & Ronald Volstad

PUBLICATIONS COMPANY

Editor: James Hill

Copyright © 1997

by CONCORD PUBLICATIONS CO.

603-609 Castle Peak Road

Kong Nam Industrial Building

10/F, B1, Tsuen Wan

New Territories, Hong Kong

We welcome authors who can help
expand our range of books. If you
would like to submit material,
please feel free to contract us.

We are always on the look-out for new,
unpublished photos for this series.
If you have photos or slides or
information you feel may be useful to
future volumes, please send them to us
for possible future publication.
Full photo credits will be given upon
publication.

ISBN 962-361-624-4

printed in Hong Kong

Though this book is not meant to be a detailed history of Nazi Germany, a certain familiarity with the political climate of pre-World War Two Germany and the rise of the Nazi regime is helpful in understanding the origins of the armed branch of the SS — the Waffen-SS.

During the 1920s and 1930s, Bavaria was a scene of political unrest in which many political parties competed for control of the government. One group, the German Workers' Party (DAP), was growing in popularity. In 1920 a World War One veteran, Adolf Hitler, became the leader of the party, changing its name to the National Socialist German Workers' Party (NSDAP), more commonly referred to as the Nazi Party. A special strong-arm unit was organized from within the party to prevent disruption of its meetings. This group of toughs was given the title of Sturmabteilung (Storm Detachment), or SA.

Hitler segregated out a sub-unit of SA men to be his personal bodyguard, which by 1929 had become known as the Schutzstaffel (Protection Squad), or simply the SS. Command of the SS was given to Heinrich Himmler, an unimpressive man who was to remain faithfully subservient to Hitler until 1945. In 1931, Ernst Röhm, an early member of the Nazi Party, became Chief-of-Staff of the SA. By 1933 Hitler was becoming increasingly uncomfortable with the anti-military posturing of Röhm and the unruly behavior of the brown-shirted members of the SA.

Having been appointed Chancellor of Germany in 1933, the ambitious Hitler was wary of the potential political problems the SA created. Under Reichsführer Himmler, the SS continued to grow in number. Along with the growth in size, there existed an increase in the divergence of the philosophies of the SS and the SA. After German President Hindenburg died in August 1933, Hitler combined the offices of Chancellor and President and became absolute ruler of Germany. In June 1934, he ordered a blood purge against the SA and its leadership, including Ernst Röhm, which was carried out by the SS, for the most part. 'The Night of the Long Knives', as the days of slaughter were termed, marked the independence of the SS from the permanently weakened SA.

From 1934 to 1939, the realm of influence of the SS expanded ominously. By 1939, the SS had a secret police branch (Gestapo), a security force and a militarized unit known as the Verfügungstruppe (which became the Waffen-SS in 1940). It is important to remember that the primary concern of the SS was not the defense and security of Germany, but rather personal loyalty to Adolf Hitler and his ideals.

Though the forces in the Waffen-SS were trained to serve as a military police force to quell civilian uprising and counter-revolution, they were not originally intended for traditional military service. But by the beginning of World War Two in 1939 they had received enough training to qualify certain elements to participate to a small extent in the Blitzkrieg operations in Poland, France and the Balkans. By the middle of 1941, troops from the Waffen-SS had been drawn from a number of sources. The first regiment was composed of members of Hitler's bodyguard regiment, Leibstandarte SS Adolf Hitler. Three smaller regiments — Deutschland, Germania and Der Führer — were combined into the Das Reich Divison. Since Himmler held the position of Chief of the German Police, he was able to create divisions from among the Totenkopf (Death's Head) guards that manned his concentration camps and from the Polizei (police) units. After the success of the Blitzkrieg, Nordic men from the conquered northern European nations volunteered to form the Wiking (Viking) Division. These four divisions of the Waffen-SS participated in Hitler's ill-fated invasion of the Soviet Union, suffering 30,000 casualties by November 1941.

By the middle of 1943, the Waffen-SS had passed through the refiner's fire of wartime combat. While the behavior of the SS troops (e.g., the extermination squads) often was influenced by their origins as a small political unit designed to protect the Führer and enforce Nazi philosophies, the Waffen-SS did manage to develop into a fighting force that earned the respect of both enemy troops and (however grudgingly) Germany's regular army.

ACKNOWLEDGEMENTS
All photographs published in this book are from: Military Institute of History; Central Military Archives; Military Photo Agency; Central Photo Archives; and the author's collection. I would like to thank Tomasz Kopanski, Slawek Gonera and the crews of the mentioned institutions for their help, support and patience.

Long before Hitler's infamous Schutzstaffel or Protection Squad (which is more widely recognized by the initials SS) came and organized, there were already SS-type men in Germany, men with guard-dog mentalities who believed that true men should sacrifice themselves in battle for the ideals of the Nazi Party and its leader, Adolf Hitler. These people could be quite barbaric, partly due to the fact that the intellectual life of the Second Reich had become outdated by the early twentieth century. The group of men seen here are 'soldiers' belonging to Stosstrupp Hitler, Hitler's personal bodyguard, who were photographed in Munich in September 1923. Judging from the rows of campaign ribbons on their chests, a few of them appear to be real patriots who fought with determination during the First World War. At the far left is the first commander of the unit, Joseph Berchtold. The man carrying the Imperial War flag is another leader, Julius Schreck. Behind him is Ulrich Graf, who would intercept a bullet shot at Hitler during the November Putsch in Munich on 9 November 1923.

Adolf Hitler prepares to bless SS and NSDAP (National Socialist German Workers', or Nazi, Party) flags with the 'power' from the Blutfahne or Blood Flag during the party meeting in November 1926. This flag was carried during Hitler's failed attempt to overthrow the government in Munich on 9 November 1923. Viewed by the Nazis as a kind of sacred relic, the bloodstained banner played a major part in later flag consecration ceremonies.

A column of SS men march through Berlin to a stadium in the Doeberitz area on 11 August 1933. The troops out front are clothed in the early all-black uniform similar to what members of the Reichswehr wore. Those in the background wear the first formal uniform of the SS: black breeches and caps, black ties, and brown shirts. The similarity to the early Nazi party SA (Sturmabteilung - Storm Detachment) uniform is readily apparent. The banner above the pillars reads: " The First Schutzstaffel Parade of Gruppe Ost (Group East) in Berlin 11, 12, 13 August 33". It is written in Gothic script, of course, since that style of writing was very Germanic. The inscription begins with the well-known SS insignia, two Sig-Runes (each a symbol of victory), and ends with the national eagle. The use of mythic Old Norse script was popular with the Nazi leaders, particularly SS leader Heinrich Himmler.

At the Gruppe Ost gathering in Berlin, Ernst Röhm (with arm raised) inspects a line of SS men. With him is Himmler (second from left), who was quite a friend of his in the early 1920s. However, during 'The Night of the Long Knives' Reichsführer Himmler sided with Hitler against him. Left of Himmler is Kurt Daluege, commander of the Berlin SS. Note the older trooper in the line of brown-shirted SS men (fifth from right). Obviously, the Great War, during which he won the Eisernenkreuz (Iron Cross), did not end for him in November 1918.

Whether a friend of Himmler's or not, Ernst Röhm was the first highly placed victim of Himmler's SS. Röhm's military ambitions and communist sympathies brought him into conflict with Hitler in July 1934, and he did not survive. Here Röhm rides horseback in review of SA troops in the company of mounted SA officers and an SS man at the Tempelhof airport in Berlin in 1933, almost a year before the purge of the SA. According to the contemporary press, there were about 81,000 SA men assembled on this occasion.

Hitler and high-ranking officers of the NSDAP and Wehrmacht arrive at the funeral of Paul von Hindenburg. Behind Hitler are Hermann Göring and Defense Minister Werner von Blomburg. To the right and left of these officials are SS men from Leibstandarte SS Adolf Hitler (LAH), the Führer's personal bodyguard regiment. Their helmets exhibit the old-style markings of the tri-color Wehrmacht emblem on the left side and, on the right, a white SS symbol on a white-outlined shield that lacks an upper left corner. Everyone wears a black mourning armband. Note that the SS men wear theirs over the standard red/white/black swastika armbands.

An SS motorcycle team is seen here during a rally at the Doberitz camp in the middle of the 1930s. Clearly visible are the old-style collar patches on their uniforms. These bear the inscription "Ost", indicating Gruppe Ost. The SS officials attached great importance to any form of sport, particularly those like motorcycling that could be useful on the battlefield.

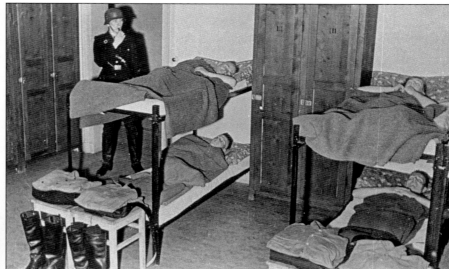

Not long after Hitler came to power, the SS began to receive state funding, so it was quickly able to expand and strengthen itself. Thanks to this money, two SS officer training schools were established at Bad Tolz and Braunschweig, where cadets were really put through the mill. Their day began at 6:00 a.m., the moment of reveille that is seen in this photo.

One of the ski champions of the SS skiers team from Gruppe Mitte, who was photographed during an NSDAP competition in February 1937. SS sportsmen always competed dressed in their SS uniform. If that was not possible, they wore SS symbols on their sports clothes.

The first duty of every cadet at the SS training school was to fall out for assembly. During the ceremony the SS flag, which was a simple black banner featuring white lightening-bolt SS runes, was raised. The photo illustrates the two types of uniform, black and gray, worn by the cadets.

As the 1930s progressed, elements of the SS began to be trained and organized more like a branch of the military. Here a Waffen-SS private, dressed in the field gray uniform of the regular army, steadies himself with his 7.92mm Mauser rifle as he adjusts a small two-dimensional model of a Pz.Kpfw. IV tank sometime in the late 1930s. Note the national eagle emblem just visible on the left sleeve. The fluted metal canister he carries contains a gas mask.

Due to imperfections in early radio traffic, the German Army still used carrier pigeons to send messages during the 1930s, and even in the 1940s during the war. The SS troops adopted this system of communication for their use, as well. Here an SS Unterscharführer (senior corporal) affixes a message to the leg of a pigeon.

Because the armed SS units were originally established as a special military police unit to deal with uprisings of armed civilians, they were introduced late to heavy weapons like antitank guns. Just when the threat of war was getting close, SS regiments began to receive guns, heavy mortars and armored vehicles. Here a 3.7cm PAK 36 antitank gun is being towed by a Krupp-Protze Kfz. 69 light truck that was specially modified for this duty.

Hitler examines the banner of the 8th Regiment of Chasseurs during his trip to conquered Poland in the middle of September 1939. The war in Poland was probably the last one in which opposing armies fought to capture banners on the battlefield. In the background is Himmler (looking away), who is wearing a field gray uniform with the white-trimmed black collar patches of Reichsführer-SS.

Many people in the 1930s, Germans and non-Germans alike, held the opinion that the SS was a positive force, especially compared to the wild and unpredictable SA organization. The SS men were more disciplined and had a more serious demeanor so, at least from a political standpoint, they were a more acceptable group than the SA. It makes sense, then, that they could be seen throughout Germany during all of the NSDAP rallies serving as special guards for the Nazi leaders. This photo shows Rudolf Hess, Hitler's right-hand man, speaking at one such rally in the late 1930s. Note the SS men, who wear a variety of headgear and uniforms, standing between the rows of SA men in the foreground and the officials on the stand (General Heinz Guderian is visible third from the right).

In autumn of 1939, in the Gdynia area of Poland, Himmler inspects lines of soldiers from one of the Totenkopf (Death's Head) guard units, which later proved themselves in combat. Other SS units failed to achieve great military success during the fighting of September 1939. One of them — the Germania regiment — even suffered a humbling defeat when it was taken by surprise by the Polish 49th Infantry Regiment during nighttime combat.

Somewhere in Warsaw during the winter of 1940, an officer of the 1.SS-Kavallerie regiment reports to Hans Frank on the readiness of his unit to be reviewed. The occupation duty in conquered Poland was the first disagreeable work in the history of the SS cavalry, but worse tasks lay ahead for the unit.

This photo is often described as showing action that was photographed during combat in France in May 1940, but it more probably shows an MG30(t) machine gun team from the 'Totenkopf' Division during training in the spring of 1940. Note that the soldiers are wearing camouflage smocks over their field equipment. The use of smocks was preferred before the war and only in the first two years of combat because they proved somewhat impractical during battle.

Columns of motorized SS troops travel through a city in western Europe during the advance toward France. SS units did not experience defeat in France like they had in Poland, but they suffered higher casualty rates — higher than the Wehrmacht units. These enormous losses, which became the trademark of the SS throughout the entire war, were not known to most people. The most surprising thing about it is that Hitler and Himmler were glad about these losses, probably due to their propagandistic value.

An SS-Oberscharführer (color sergeant) familiarizes himself with some French heavy artillery shells that were captured by his unit. Some of the interesting aspects of his uniform are the goggles and gloves, as well as the camouflage cover secured to his helmet.

A truckload of SS troops bask in the adulation they receive from their fellow Germans as they return from waging war against the Third Reich's most hated enemy - France. Once again camouflage covers are visible on their helmets. The SS troops were the first combat unit in the world at that time to issue camouflage cloth as a standard piece of a soldier's equipment.

Here an SS-Oberscharführer from the 'Germania' regiment talks with a French policeman. Only a few short months after the June 1940 fall of France, friendly cooperation existed between the SS and the French police to solve issues of mutual concern, for example, the perceived 'Jewish threat'. Post-war history claims that the police were forced by the Nazis to assist in their dirty work. This photo provides an excellent study of Waffen-SS uniform details such as collar insignia, unit title cuffband, national eagle emblem on the sleeve, and white metal death's head and national eagle insignia on the field cap.

Throughout nearly the entire year following the collapse of France, all of the SS units received combat tactic training and new armaments, such as these two Panzerjäger I tank destroyers, which were equipped with 4.7cm Czech-made guns. Photographed on 25 February 1941, the new vehicles, which belong to the 'LAH' brigade, are being inspected by Wehrmacht Gen.-Oberst. von Blaskowitz (second from left, wearing the Knight's Cross around his neck) and 'LAH' commander SS-Obergruppenführer (General) Dietrich, whose profile is to the camera.

Regional political leader Gauleiter Bohle receives the salute of the Ehrenkompanie (honorary company) of militarized police who were employed to carry out the most dirty assignments in the field during WWII. This sort of force was under the command of the SS and consisted of second-class recruits and reservists. Despite their weakness—or perhaps because of it—they earned a reputation as butchers of prisoners of war and civilians.

Motorcyclists take a brief respite in the woods before continuing their advance in Greece. They wear the motorcyclist's waterproof coat.

The 'LAH' (expanded to brigade strength after the French campaign, but still kept the standarte designation) proved to be a first-class unit during the fighting in Greece and in the Balkans. Here a motorcycle unit from the 'LAH' reconnaissance battalion travels down a road in Greece along the western slope of the Arakynthos towards the town of Mesolongion in April 1941.

A Kfz. 15 Horch signals car negotiates difficult terrain during the campaign in Greece. Along with the rest of the German troops who were being mobilized to invade Russia, the motorized Waffen-SS units had been rerouted from their original destination (the Russian border) to help fight in Greece.

The swift advance of the German strike force against the Greeks resulted in the capture of many prisoners. Here several Greek prisoners file down a dirt road in between some German reconnaissance vehicles — an Sd.Kfz. 222 (foreground), an Sd.Kfz. 223 (left background) and an Sd.Kfz. 232 (right background).

A Horch heavy vehicle displaying a white flag carries elements of the 'LAH' passes a crowd of Greek civilians. Note the unit emblem painted on the front of the hood of the vehicle — an unusual location.

Rending the air with the blast from their sIG 33 gun, an artillery crew from an SS regiment (probably 'LAH') opens fire on Greek troops that have taken advantage of the terrain to hide from sight. Note the position of each member of the crew and how they protect their ears from the explosive noise.

Working their way along a mountain side to remain as protected as possible, a heavy mortar team takes advantage of a lull in the fighting to put their weapon into position. Note that each man wears the camouflage smock commonly associated with SS troops.

Racing as quickly as possible while loaded down with the weight of a heavy mortar and its ammunition, two members of the SS mortar team run to catch up with the rest of the team already across the road. Of interest is the way the mortar is folded for transport.

The gunner and loader of the heavy mortar crew set up their weapon and make the necessary adjustments so that it is zeroed in on the enemy fortification. Soon the SS men will be ready to get down to business.

This photo shows the timely arrival of a 15cm howitzer and its removal from its tractor. The location is one of an infinite number of mountain roads that were so useful to the Germans in the movement of men and machinery during the fighting in Greece.

With their 15cm howitzer in position and loaded, the Waffen-SS gun crew opens fire on a distant target. The watchful eye of the gun team's observer will direct the fire until the enemy troops are scattered or killed. Note the ramrod held by the artilleryman at the left.

An 8.8cm Flak gun joins in the action and responds to harassing fire from the enemy. Although known for its antiaircraft capabilities, the German Army often used the '88' to deadly effect against massed ground forces.

This photo shows SS troops preparing a 15cm howitzer to go into action from its position on a mountain road. Note how the ammunition is piled up rather haphazardly. Of further interest are the long wicker containers in which the ammunition is stored.

A Sd.Kfz. 222 reconnaissance vehicle, with the name 'Alter Schultz' (Old Schultz) painted on its armor, easily traverses the uneven Greek mountain terrain in pursuit of enemy soldiers that have been forced to retreat before the pursuing SS troops. Over rocks and down inclines, the strike force advances toward its eventual defeat of the Greek Army.

After the defeat of the Greek Army, fighting continued against British resistance in southern Greece. While arriving at the Gulf of Patras, the leading motorcycles from the 'LAH' recce battalion receive uncertain greetings from local Greek civilians as they travel along a seaside road to the harbor village of Nafpaktos.

After arriving at Nafpaktos, the SS men commandeered some boats to use as landing craft to transport themselves and their vehicles. The first wave consisted of two boats loaded with about eight or ten BMW motorcycles with sidecars and a 3.7cm PAK gun.

Two members of the Aufklärung Abteilung (reconnaissance battalion) of the 'LAH' secure a Nazi flag to a convenient spot where it will be visible for air identification purposes. The unit was then ready to sail to the Peloponnesus in southern Greece with a supply of ammunition. Note the difference in appearance between the older, faded and the newer camouflage smocks worn by these men. The weapon resting on the flag is the familiar 9mm MP40 Schmeisser machine pistol.

The Waffen-SS men who crossed the Gulf of Patras on the first two boats were ready to engage the enemy, who could have been dug-in near the beaches of the Peloponnesus. The British, who were completely surprised, offered no serious resistance, however.

After reaching the Peloponnesus, the SS men from the battalion commanded by SS-Sturmbannführer (Major) Hurt Meyer continued to press forward. About 7:00am in the morning they reached Olympia, the mythical mountain home of the Greek gods.

The pursuit of the British Army did not end on the Peloponnesus, but the soldiers of 'LAH' traveled to the northwest side of the island, specifically to the Olympia area, where the lead squad enjoyed a much-needed rest. Here is a photo of an official ceremony in that region. Featured prominently in the photo is the Reich Service flag.

'LAH' troops sit along the edges of a reservoir in Olympia during a break from front-line duty. No doubt the officer at the left is taking this opportunity to motivate his men with a rousing political speech about the important work they are performing in Greece.

In the early part of a war that would eventually engulf the entire world, troops belonging to the first squads of the 'LAH' brigade to reach Olympia pose for souvenir photos at the very spot where the fire originated that blazed in Berlin at the 1936 Olympic games.

Not all the troops of the 'LAH' reconnaissance unit were interested in enjoying a free sight-seeing tour of one of the most interesting places in Greece. Some of them preferred to get some sleep when the opportunity arose, even when no bed was available.

Only a few of the 'LAH' troops received the Ritterkreuz (Knight's Cross) for their performance during the campaign in Greece. One of them, SS-Obersturmführer (First Lieutenant) Gerd Pleiss, commander of the 1st company in the 'LAH', is seen here at the far left with soldiers from his unit, who have been decorated with the Iron Cross. Pleiss, who won the award on 20 April 1941, was killed in action in Russia on 17 November 1941 during the fighting in the Rostov on the Don region.

After a three-week delay in plans that was caused by the short campaign in Greece, Hitler finally unleashed his armies against Russia in Operation 'Barbarossa' in June of 1941. Here members of a Waffen-SS reconnaissance squad move deep into Soviet territory in their heavy sidecar-equipped motorcycle. Note how 'stick' grenades have been secured wherever they possibly could be.

Squads equipped with motorcycles were the fastest and most mobile elements of the SS formations. Here two SS men set out on a mission with a Soviet POW. Neither German seems to be armed, while the prisoner holds a spade. Apparently they feel that the POW poses no threat. Notice the tear in the camouflage fabric covering the driver's helmet.

These soldiers belonging to the 'LAH' Division (refitted and renamed SS Division Leibstandarte SS Adolf Hitler just before the invasion of Russia) were photographed in the heat of battle somewhere in a Ukrainian field. Their vehicle is a Sd.Kfz. 6/2 armed with a 3.7cm antiaircraft gun and equipped with an ammunition trailer that bears the 'LAH' Division badge. Note the way in which the spare tires and ammo are carried on the gun platform.

This Soviet prisoner photo is shown here digging up land mines that were left behind by the retreating Red Army. A squad of SS troops, led by a Sturmbannführer (major) wearing a Knight's Cross, examine his work intently as they file past.

The war against Russia was considered the most important mission in the history of the SS. It was the culmination of the ideological conflict between Nazism and 'Jewish Bolshevism', as the Nazis referred to communism in their propaganda. It was also a risky business. Seated a safe distance from his burning BA-10 heavy armored car, a slightly burned Russian crew, who managed to escape the vehicle before it exploded, receives solace from a member of the 'LAH'.

Members of a reconnaissance squad of the 'LAH' Division clash with 'Bolsheviks' in one of many August skirmishes in the Uman area of Ukraine. Once again we see the 'LAH' key-in-the-shield unit badge on the Sd.Kfz. 222 armored car.

This photo shows SS men of 'LAH' engaged in street fighting in one of the Uman villages. While soldiers from the motorcycle units check each of the houses, Sd.Kfz. 222s press ahead past abandoned trucks in the search for enemy forces.

A column of machine gun troops from the 'Totenkopf' Division, which was originally made up of former concentration camp guards, march down a road in the northwestern sector of the Russian Front in the summer of 1941. The gunners are armed with MG30(t) machine guns and, together with other members of the machine gun teams, carry special cartridge pouches designed to carry ammunition for their weapons.

In July 1941, the Germans reached the so-called 'Stalin Line', the line of fortifications built on the old Polish-Soviet border, where systems of strong bunkers were located. Pictured here is one such bunker being inspected by SS troops after its destruction and capture.

This Red Army artillery unit ran out of luck — it was intercepted by SS men by surprise and captured intact. Visible in the photo are a single gun, a 122mm D-20 Model 38 howitzer, and an STZ-5-type tractor. The SS units would happily put these captured items to good use, eventually giving the howitzer to a lesser-quality SS unit.

This is just one of dozens of vehicle graveyards left behind in the wake of the Waffen-SS units as they advanced into Russia in August 1941. From the obvious lack of sophistication of this equipment, it is no wonder they were no match for the German troops.

This SS trophy, an early series Russian BT-7 tank that has been equipped with a radio, was discovered in a ditch by the German troops. It is interesting to note that the seemingly overweight man with his hand on the aerial may negate some claims that the SS units still had a strict recruitment policy in 1939.

A two-man machine-gun team let loose a burst from their MG34 during a firefight in Russia. Both Waffen-SS men have equipment and uniforms typical of this period in the war, with the possible exception of the camouflaged shelter half or Zeltbahn on the back of the soldier at right. This was rarely seen during the first part of the war.

Hard work played as big a part in the pursuit of Soviet troops in the summer of 1941 as any 'glorious' battles did. Here several SS men struggle to move an ammunition trailer from a sunken road up to higher ground.

Here SS men engage themselves in a team effort to move a motorcycle and sidecar across a demolished bridge. While no medals would be handed out for the duty performed here, it was essential nonetheless in the overall goal of swift German domination of the Soviet Union.

SS-Schütze, Standarte 'Germania', SS-Verfügungstruppe, Western Front 1940

This rifleman wears the M1938 type camouflage smock in 'plane tree' material. The smock was still in limited issue at time of the campaign in the west, while the helmet cover was in much wider distribution.

This early smock was originally intended to be worn over the personal equipment, thus the very low elastic waist band and the vertical access slits. In practice, the equipment was almost worn over the smock. The neck of the smock was fitted with elastic but this proved to be unnecessary.

The smock is worn over the standard field gray uniform and the footwear is the original tall leather marching boots. Photos show some members of this unit wearing neck scarves of checked material.

The equipment is that of a typical German infantryman but note the absence of the leather support straps. These also were in limited issue.

Note the gas cape pouch worn on the web strap of the gas mask canister. These early pouches were made from rubberized canvas.

Also carried is a 27mm flare pistol slung in a holster on his left hip. The leather flare pouch is slung on the right.

He is armed with the standard Karabiner 98K and has an M1920 stick grenade tucked into his belt.

The only insignia visible is his right collar tabs bearing the SS runes and the regimental of 'Standarte Germania'.

VOLSTAD97

SS-Scharführer, SS Panzer-Grenadier-Division 'Totenkopf', Eastern Front

This NCO is a typical image of the Waffen SS soldier on the Eastern Front until 1943.

Like the distinctive helmet cover, the camouflage smock was now common wear for combat troops. This smock is the M1940 type, which deleted the elastic in the collar. These early smocks were frequently worn with the skirt tucked up under the waist elastic. The cuffs were also treated similarly as in the other figure. The 'palm' camouflage pattern was very common of the M38 and M40 smocks.

The uniform is the standard early war field gray pattern but the boots now have a shortened shaft.

His equipment is typical of a German NCO including 6x30 binoculars and a M1935 dispatch case. The leather support straps were in broad issue by 1942 and are hooked into the rings of the canvas pouches for the MP38/40.

His collar shows the only visible insignia with the right tab displaying an early type of 'Totenkopf' and the left tab showing the rank of SS-Scharführer. The collar is edged with gray NCO 'tress'.

His weapons are the MP40 and a pair of M1920 stick grenades.

VOLSTAD 97

These Russian soldiers fell into the hands of the SS after they were captured by a German patrol. The SS-Untersturmführer (2nd lieutenant) at right looks rather menacing, so the fate of the Soviets could be grim. Even if they happened to survive this meeting, their chances for survival were slim. About 35% of Red Army POWs died or were killed in German camps, most of them during the winter of 1941/42 when conditions were the toughest.

Soviet prisoners receive instruction from their SS captor. Contrary to some beliefs, front-line SS units were not necessarily more brutal to prisoners than the Wehrmacht units. Since they were involved in heavy fighting at the front, it is arguable that they were unavailable for at least some of the 'dirty work' attributed to them. A lot of Russian POWs captured by SS troops survived their captivity without problems. Their real troubles began in the rear areas where second-line units of the SS searched the camps for Jews and communist leaders. If they survived this purge, they had to fight for their lives in POW camps during the early stages of the war because the Wehrmacht was not prepared to handle such large numbers of POWs.

Dressed in a greatcoat and cap, this captured Soviet soldier is leading SS troops, who carry a variety of weapons, into combat position against other Russian soldiers. Note that the SS man at the extreme left is armed with a Mauser rifle that is equipped to fire rifle grenades.

Nazi propaganda claimed that Germany was handing down the torch of civilization to the nations in the East and that their occupation was a secular mission of the German nation. This photo of two SS men, who are apparently voluntarily repairing an archaic Soviet farming machine, illustrates this propaganda position. There is no way of knowing, however, if the owners of this machine were still alive at the time this photo was taken or if they ever benefited from Nazi Germany's 'torch'.

Dug into position near a barn, SS men wait for the approach of the enemy troops. Apparently the time for fighting is close since the German troops exhibit no interest in the potential dinner rooting around at the extreme right. Note that the SS man at left is using ammunition from an MG34 belt for his Mauser rifle.

The fight has already commenced for this machine-gun team. The interesting weapon they man looks like the aviation model of the 7.92mm MG15 machine-gun, which is mounted on an MG34 stand, being used as a heavy machine-gun.

An SS sniper takes up a position along a fence as he keeps his sight trained on movement at the opposite end of the village. The absence of Y-strap leather equipment suspenders may indicate that these men belong to a motorcycle troop of a reconnaissance unit.

Within the same fenced area of a Russian farmhouse as seen in the photo of the sniper, Waffen-SS soldiers go on the offensive with an MG34 machine gun set up on a Dreifuss 34 antiaircraft tripod mount. If the sniper fire is not adequate, a few bursts from this machine gun will suppress any enemy activity.

Another MG34 machine gun team goes into action in Russia, this time using a tripod for long-range firing. The soldiers must have been engaged in a lengthy duel since at least one ammunition box is already empty. The firepower of the German Army, including the SS, was one of the important factors in overwhelming the Red Army throughout the entire war. When facing a German machine gun team supplied with plenty of ammunition, the Soviet units had a difficult time, especially since their own supply of ammunition was often inadequate.

Pioneers from the 'Totenkopf' Division put the finishing touches on a pontoon bridge for divisional 'Blitz' trucks near another bridge that was improvised for the use of the infantry. Note the death's-head unit badge painted on the fender of the truck at right. The 'Totenkopf' Division fought in the northern sector of the Eastern Front, ending their service there in 1941 in the Demyansk pocket. The unit began Operation 'Barbarossa' in an unlucky way — they were unpleasantly surprised by troops of the Soviet 42nd Armored Division in the Dagda area and lost many soldiers. It would not be their last misfortune. After the first 16 days of fighting, soldiers of the 2nd regiment were used to replace high losses in the 1st and 3rd regiments.

Loaded with SS troops, an Opel Blitz truck from the 'Wiking' Division travels down a road in a Ukrainian village. Though carefully camouflaged, a 3.7cm PAK antitank gun sits in plain sight in position in the middle of a side road outside the village.

SS trucks cross a more rigid and permanent bridge as the push into Russia continues. These heavy transport vehicles are marked on their fenders with the rounded swastika emblem of the Wiking (Viking) Division. This SS unit, composed of Aryan-looking Danes, Norwegians, Dutchmen and Belgians, was deployed in the southern sector of the front during the summer of 1941.

Wreckage and debris, the remains of a Red Army motorized column wiped out in battle by the Germans, serve to notify everyone that the German Army had passed through the area. Scenes like this were commonplace all around the western part of Russia during the first three months of the war there.

SS troops were free to travel this road after rear-echelon troops spent a few hours cleaning up the debris and pushing demolished vehicles off to the side of the road. However, as successful as the German advance was in the early months of fighting, time was to work against the Germans as autumn and winter approached.

During their advance eastward, German soldiers came across countless bridges that had been destroyed either by the Luftwaffe or the Soviets. Thanks to their initiative and zeal, the troops managed to negotiate the watery obstacles somehow. Here an SS machine-gun team dressed in mottled camouflaged employ an improvised footbridge to cross a stream.

Troops from the 'Polizei' Division storm an enemy-held riverbank with the use of a boat 'borrowed' from a Russian village. SS men of this division wore camouflage smocks and uniforms with SS markings, but they could be recognized by the Wehrmacht collar patches. The soldier in the foreground carries a Czech-made MG30(t) machine gun in his right hand. This weapon was commonly used by the sub-units of the SS and police formations.

Another means of crossing rivers was the pontoon boat, this one being armed with a 3.7cm PAK gun from an antiaircraft battery, most likely from the 'Das Reich' Division. Note the netting secured to the gun shield by ammunition boxes. SS-Division 'Das Reich', which was composed members of the original Verfügungstruppe (reserve unit) and some former 'Totenkopf' troops, fought very well in the last days of June 1941, when its troops successfully tangled with the Red Army's 20th Motorized Corps. While approaching the Dnieper River, they encountered their Soviet counterpart — a NKVD security force unit.

This photo illustrates a more inventive use of the pontoon for river crossings. Two pontoons have been connected to a bridge section and turned into a makeshift transport craft propelled by the muscles of SS men with oars. The craft in the foreground carries a 3.7cm PAK gun and a motorcycle and sidecar. The one in the background is being loaded with a heavy troop transport automobile. Elements of the 'Das Reich' Division captured the first bridgehead on the Dnieper River on July 4, 1941.

The remains of a Red Army KV-1 heavy tank that successfully fled from advancing SS troops only to become bogged down in the mud after the bridge it was crossing collapsed under its weight. It was eventually destroyed by the Germans when they came upon it.

34

Crew members of the SS-Sturmartillerie Abteilung (assault artillery battalion) paint the sixth victory ring on the gun barrel of their StuG III. Nicknamed 'Ursel', the StuG is covered with a patchy paint job and adorned with the 'Totenkopf' skull emblem, which was used by the StuG battery in the 'Totenkopf' Division.

SS-Obergruppenführer (General) Josef 'Sepp' Dietrich (left) and SS-Sturmbannführer (Major) Meyer watch the 'LAH' Division fight around Perekop in October 1941. The commander of the German formation storming the Crimea, Gen. von Sodenstern, was unhappy with 'LAH', but he was forced to accept this unit under his command.

Here we see a motorcycle trooper performing his duty as a messenger between the SS regimental staff and the battalions. Despite the use of radio and telephones, the two-wheeled messenger was still very useful during the first part of the war.

Schwimmwagen amphibious vehicles belonging to a reconnaissance unit produce a cloud of dust as they travel along a road during the German advance in the Soviet Union. Germany probably had the finest land reconnaissance sub-units used in World War Two, and they were most fruitfully employed on the Eastern Front.

This close-up shows a three-man Schwimmwagen team wearing typical SS camouflage. The skull on the driver's right collar patch identifies these men as members of the 'Totenkopf' Division. They were photographed driving through the Baltic states on their way into the Leningrad area.

This series of four photos depicts a pair of SS men from the 'LAH' Division making sure that these two Soviet armored vehicles no longer pose a threat to the German Army. The large tank in the background is a KV-2 heavy tank, many of which were abandoned by their crews due to mechanical problems. The smaller vehicle is a BA-10 armored car. The ransacked suitcase visible in the second and third photos indicates that these AFVs have been vacant for a while and probably posed no threat. Still, the action shots made for good propaganda back home.

SS troops advance across the wide expanse of western Russia, obviously curious about the photographic unit they are passing. At the right is a Horch heavy cross-country vehicle towing a 3.7cm PAK antitank gun. Following the gun is a captured Soviet truck that was manufactured under license of the Ford automobile manufacturing company. The same (or very similar) types of Ford trucks were produced for the Wehrmacht in Germany and France and used against the Soviets in Russia and, later, the Americans in France. Because the Germans were so familiar with these vehicles, many of the captured Soviet trucks were put to use, at least on a temporary basis.

Following behind the front-line SS regiments were the troops that handled the dirty work for the SS, such as the extermination of Jews, communists and members of anti-German movements. There were four Einsatzgruppen (action teams) and three SS brigades involved in this activity. Their operations grew quickly to be among the bloodiest of such behavior in twentieth century military history. As we can see from the eagle-and-laurel insignia on the Panzerspährwagen P204(f) armored car in this photo, the Einsatzgruppen soldiers (visible in the background) were sometimes assisted by troops from the police units, including some from SS-Division 'Polizei', which saw action in the northwestern part of the Russian Front.

Members of an Einsatzgruppe, performing a task that was routine for them, shoot wounded soldiers from a Red Army armored unit equipped with OT-133 tanks fitted with flame-throwers. Soldiers belonging to Einsatzgruppen are often easily recognized in photos by their weapons — an MP28, for example — and because they 'fought' without field equipment and camouflage smocks. By the end of 1941, Einsatzgruppen had killed about 400,000 people, most of them Jews and a small number of partisans.

Almost from the very beginning of Operation 'Barbarossa', SS soldiers had to fight skirmishes with small groups of 'Bolshevik desperadoes' who used the varied terrain to resist the 'Fascist beasts'. Here an SS unit is seen chasing a small group of Soviet soldiers, the only survivors of their defeated unit, who are still attempting to fight off the Germans or break through to the Soviet lines.

An SS man closes in on a burning building during anti-partisan action in a cornfield somewhere in Russia. Combat with partisan troops in the summer and autumn of 1941 was rare, so the extermination units of the SS could perform their jobs without any major problems. Another reason for this is that the real occupation work was performed by eight police battalions with 3,200 soldiers supported by about 20,000 policemen from the ORPO, the uniformed police unit. All such units were weaker than the well-equipped and well-organized SS troops, and were more exposed to partisan assault. As a result, by April 1942 the ORPO had lost 4,000 men in anti-partisan activity, while the units engaged in extermination work suffered minor losses.

Another shot of similar anti-partisan activity. The soldiers in the foreground belong to Fegelein's SS cavalry brigade, which was also involved in extermination work. Note the style of wearing camouflage smocks. The soldier at right even has his belt and gas-mask canister covered with a special piece of the camouflage material. The soldier at left has a smock printed with the 'palm tree' pattern, while both of the others have dotted 'plane tree'-pattern smocks.

The barely visible cuff titles worn by this soldier identify him as a military policeman from the Feldgendarmerie unit of the 'LAH' Division. He is shown examining an AVS Model 36 rifle captured from a Soviet partisan taken prisoner during an anti-partisan operation. There is no doubt that this photo was the last one taken of this Soviet man. Most likely he was killed in the field or in a concentration camp not long after this photo was taken. Along with over four million Red Army soldiers, almost one million Soviets from paramilitary or partisan groups were taken prisoner by the Germans. After being captured, they had a much smaller chance of surviving life in a prison camp than the regular soldiers from the Red Army.

Having been issued no protective winter clothing, the SS troops suffered from the inclement weather during the Russian winter just as badly the ill-supplied Wehrmacht troops. Here a Waffen-SS soldier wearing a white smock inspects a snow-covered Soviet KV-1 heavy tank. Designed simply to provide camouflage in the snow, the smock offered no relief from the bitter winter chill.

When the winter of 1941 arrived, the SS units were the only German land force that was even partly prepared for the bitter weather. Here an MG34 team zeros in on the enemy using a Lafette 34 sight, which permitted firing at ranges as distant as 2,000 meters (2,186 yards). The gunner is wearing civilian-style winter clothing over a standard uniform, but the other soldier relies solely on a greatcoat for warmth.

SS-Sturmbannführer (Major) Wilfried Richter from the 'Totenkopf' Division, who won fame during the fighting around the village of Kalitkino in the Demyansk pocket in the winter of 1941/42 when he led a group of SS men in a counterattack against an enemy armored unit. During the fight the Soviets, who were beaten off, lost six out of ten of the tanks that were in action. Richter was decorated with the Knight's Cross on 22 April 1942.

Another SS hero of the Winterkampf (Winter War) 1941/42, SS-Sturmbannführer (Major) August Dieckmann, the commander of the 'Germania' regiment, who was decorated with the Knight's Cross on 24 April 1942. An SS member since 1934, Dieckmann was later made commander of the 'Wiking' Division and led it well on the Miusfront in 1943.

SS-Oberführer (Brigadier-General) Hermann Fegelein, commander of the 'Florian Geyer' cavalry division, which he commanded from its formation when it participated in extermination work. He was decorated with the Knight's Cross on Hitler's order on 2 March 1942 for his service during the heavy fighting of winter 1941/42. It was also on Hitler's order, however, that he was executed in Berlin on 29 April 1945.

In July 1942, an SS commander congratulates soldiers of the 'Totenkopf' Division on their receipt of decorations earned for bravery in combat during the fighting of early 1942. Their chevrons and collar patches indicate that all the men share the rank of SS-Sturmann (lance corporal) except for the SS-Schütze (private) who stands second from left and the SS-Rottenführer (corporal) at far right.

The year 1942 was a quiet one for the Waffen-SS in Russia. The 'Polizei' Division sent some of its troops to fight in areas in the rear against partisans while the 'Das Reich' Division enjoyed a long vacation in France. Only the 'LAH' and 'Wiking' divisions took part in the fighting in the southern sector of the Eastern Front. Soon afterward, both 'LAH' and 'Totenkopf' were also sent to France. This photo shows a machine-gun team from one of these divisions positioned in a field of sunflowers during a firefight.

In 1942 the Germans suffered much due to the increased partisan activity to the rear of the main lines. Therefore, SS and police units who had been involved in some of the extermination activity the previous year were mainly assigned to anti-partisan duty. This photo shows soldiers from these anti-partisan units in the northern sector of the Eastern Front. In the foreground are soldiers from the police units who are working together with SS men from Kavalleriedivision 'Florian Geyer'. Note the old MG08/15 machine gun being manned by a second-class squad of troops.

This close-up of soldiers belonging to either the 'LAH' or 'Wiking' Division shows the details of the MG34's Lafette sight, used for long-range marksmanship. Note the complex multicolor spot pattern on the camouflage material.

The only SS division that was involved in heavy fighting during 1942 was 'Totenkopf', which struggled in the Demyansk area up to the middle of autumn. The fighting in this area was almost stationary and the Germans ended up digging trenches. Though not too deep, they were adequate. Here an officer of the 'Totenkopf' Division runs along the shallow floor of one of the trenches. Note that he carries an MP28 — a rather atypical weapon for front-line troops at this stage of the fighting.

A highly decorated SS-Untersturmführer (second lieutenant) from the 'Totenkopf' division visits a front-line position manned by soldiers from his unit. Below his tunic pocket he wears an Iron Cross and an Assault Badge, and over his ribbons is a Close Combat Clasp. Note the absence of any combat gear strapped to the body of the man in the foreground. During stationary fighting, soldiers often did not wear their field equipment.

Dressed in a mixture of the standard uniform and camouflage gear, Waffen-SS soldiers from the 'Totenkopf' Division crouch behind an earthen wall as they wait for the order to advance into action. Note the mess tin attached to the belt of the soldier in the foreground at right.

One of the most popular antiaircraft guns used in the SS divisions was the 2cm Flak gun. It was often used against targets on land, as well — even armored ones. Here we see the crew of the Flak 38 at their battle stations preparing to put the gun into action.

One of the main factors that have contributed to success on the battlefields of modern history is good camouflage, and here is an example of some of the best. Buried beneath birch trees and straw is a barely recognizable Sd.Kfz. 251 armored personnel carrier from the 'Totenkopf' Division.

SS-Unterscharführer (Senior-Corporal) Hans Hirning of the 6th 'Totenkopf' regiment of the 'Totenkopf' Division is decorated with the Knight's Cross that he won on 2 November 1942 for his bravery in the August-September fighting. On his right sleeve is a patch that indicates that he has destroyed a tank in close-range combat. Hirning was killed during the last days of the war — on 30 April 1945. Of special interest is the 'Totenkopf' collar patch on the uniform of the soldier behind him. The skull is at a 90-degree angle from how it appears on the standard patch.

SS troops manning a 2cm Flakvierling 38 antiaircraft gun stay alert as they search for enemy aircraft flying within range of their battery. Note the victory markings on the gun shield showing they have shot down five aircraft. The crew and the gun are camouflaged with gray, which is the best color for blending in with the landscape in the late autumn and early spring in the Soviet Union.

Two Waffen-SS soldiers cautiously approach an enemy position as they make their way through their personal 'valley of death' created by T-34 tanks positioned in the 'no-man's-land' between the front lines. Making every effort to use camouflage to his best advantage, the soldier at right wears the top part of his uniform with the white side out, but has chosen to leave the gray side of his trousers showing.

A derelict Russian KV-1 heavy tank sits like a monument to death not far from a Waffen-SS machine-gun position. This nighttime photo gives a good idea of the bleak scenery that haunted the days and nights of the German and Russian troops during the winter fighting on the Eastern Front.

This SS man is far better equipped for bitter cold weather than his brothers-in-arms were during their first Russian winter. Of note is the special gray woolen hood that fits over his head and neck and ties under the chin. Such hoods also were manufactured in a camouflage material.

In early 1943, an SS sapper at the Leningrad Front presses his body close to the mushy thawing snow as he risks his life in the middle of combat to disarm a land mine. With the ground still frozen, he is unable to burrow into the earth for more protection.

Wehrmacht and SS troops plan an upcoming mission. The soldiers of the two organizations wear basically the same uniform, with only some slight differences. The men at left are dressed in reversible clothing that allows them to wear either white or gray, depending on the season and type of weather. The soldier in the foxhole at right, though, wears a white parka that is suitable only for snowy landscape.

An SS sapper races across a ditch made up of frozen earth. The disabled T-34 might have been the victim of a land mine placed by this sapper.

A typical photo of a German tank commander posing in the turret's cupola. The tank is a Pz.Kpfw. III painted in white winter camouflage and equipped with a short-barreled 5cm gun. The SS-Panzerkommandeur is also prepared for fighting in the winter landscape. Note his fur cap, the design of which was inspired by the Soviet headgear called the 'ushanka'. It was often made of rabbit fur for SS troops, but this one is a cheaper, more common version.

Often sinking up to their waists in the freshly fallen snow, the repair crew draws ever closer to the location of the damaged communication wire. Along with their equipment they carry their weapons, loaded and ready to put to use. Their white fur-lined coats provide warmth as well as much-needed camouflage.

Staying alert as they cut a path through knee-deep snow over a mountain pass, three SS men (possibly from the Leningrad Front) set out to repair some radio lines that have been damaged by enemy fire during the action in the winter of 1942/43. Note the manner in which the spool of communications wire is carried.

Armed with both a pistol and a sub-machine gun, one of the members of the communications line repair crew struggles up a steep slope. The bulkiness of his trousers and the thick coat attest to the severity of the cold weather that slows his pace and hinders the progress of his fellow soldiers.

After having discovered that the radio wire had been lacerated as a result of an explosion from a Soviet mortar round, the repair crew was able to restore communication. Here one of the well-armed SS men adjusts the stick grenade that was stuck into his belt. Note his winter clothing and his Schmeisser MP40 machine pistol.

The first Tiger tank units of the Waffen SS were issued to the heavy tank battalions of the 'LAH' and 'Das Reich' Divisions in December 1942. They went into action in February 1943 during the fighting in the Kharkov area. This Tiger is an early SS version with the old-style cupola. Note how the road wheels have been painted white. The lack of a machine gun at the front of the hull indicates that this tank is probably the command version of the Tiger.

A crew member of a Marder III tank destroyer watches a Russian T-34 tank as it smokes in the distance after having received a well-aimed hit from the German self-propelled gun. The battle for the industrial city of Kharkov, which was waged in an attempt to push back the advance made by the Russians in their offensive of November 1942-February 1943 west of Stalingrad, was the first operation for a large SS formation composed of the three original SS divisions — 'LAH', 'Totenkopf' and 'Das Reich'. The successful SS troops were commanded by Josef 'Sepp' Dietrich.

An SS NCO inspects the damage inflicted on a Soviet tank unit. The photo shows the snow-covered remains of a T-60 light tank and a T-34 medium tank. The curious soldier, who wears a two-color, two-piece winter uniform, has a green armband around his left sleeve for quick recognition.

A column of Sd.Kfz. 251 armored personnel carrier belonging to the SS-Panzerkorps, which was formed in February 1943, take a detour across a snowy field near a village in the Kharkov area. Note how much equipment (particularly knapsacks) belonging to the troops is hanging on the sides of the Hanomag halftrack.

The grim reality of war is seen here in a photo of four SS men from the SS-Panzerkorps armored unit who were killed during the heavy fighting in the Kharkov area in February 1943. During this operation, the SS-Panzerkorps lost about 10,000 soldiers killed, wounded and missing.

A PzBeobWg III observation tank belonging to the 'LAH' Division is shown here in the vicinity of Kharkov during the last fighting there in March 1943. The tank is painted in a faintly visible two-tone camouflage scheme, with dark green stripes sprayed over panzer gray, while its crew wear newly issued winter uniforms that include gray overcoats with hoods lined with white fur.

Following a winter skirmish, SS troops from the 'Totenkopf' Division amuse themselves by taking a close look at a KV-1 heavy tank that fell victim to one of their antitank rounds and then ran into a hut. Note that the cuffband on the soldier at right displays only the death's-head emblem and not the inscription of the division's name.

Using a camouflaged Zeltbahn shelter half as a protective sheet, a Waffen-SS soldier practices his barbering skills on a fellow SS man during a break in the fighting in the southern sector of the Eastern Front. Note the two different styles of 'ushanka' fur hats worn by the men. The 'barber' wears one of gray fur that is decorated with the national eagle and the skull emblem of the SS. The one worn by the soldier at right, which is of gray material with black fur, features no insignia.

With careful concentration an SS man prepares a box of egg-type Model 39 hand grenades for upcoming combat. He is wearing gray trousers from a two-part gray/white winter uniform and an old-style camouflage helmet cover. In his buttonhole he wears the ribbon for the Iron Cross 2nd Class. The national eagle on his left arm is gray on a black background. This style was introduced during the war due to the expense of the aluminum ones and because the old white eagles were too easily visible to the enemy.

SS-Obersturmbannführer (Lieutenant-Colonel) Friedrich Wilhelm Bock, commander of II.Abteilung of the artillery regiment of SS-Division 'Polizei'. He was decorated with the Knight's Cross on 1 April 1943 for the performance of artillery sub-units commanded by him at the front while resisting the advance of the Soviet troops. Later Ostubaf. Bock was commanding officer of artillery in II.SS-Panzerkorps and leader of 9.SS-Panzerdivision 'Hohenstaufen'.

The notorious SS-Obergruppenführer (General) Josef 'Sepp' Dietrich is seen here at Insbruk in 1943 at a visit to a shooting match organized by the Hitlerjugend (Hitler Youth). Around his neck the famous Waffen-SS commander wears the Knight's Cross with Oak Leaves and Swords.

While not quite as impressive as 'Sepp' Dietrich's Knight Cross, the Motor Transport Driver's Award that this SS-Rottenführer (corporal) has been given seems to please him just fine. This badge was issued to driver's who noticeably distinguished themselves while on campaign. In his buttonhole is the red ribbon with a black stripe of the 'Winter Battle in the East 1941-1942' medal. By the end of the spring of 1943, the troops of the SS divisions had proven their worth in combat.